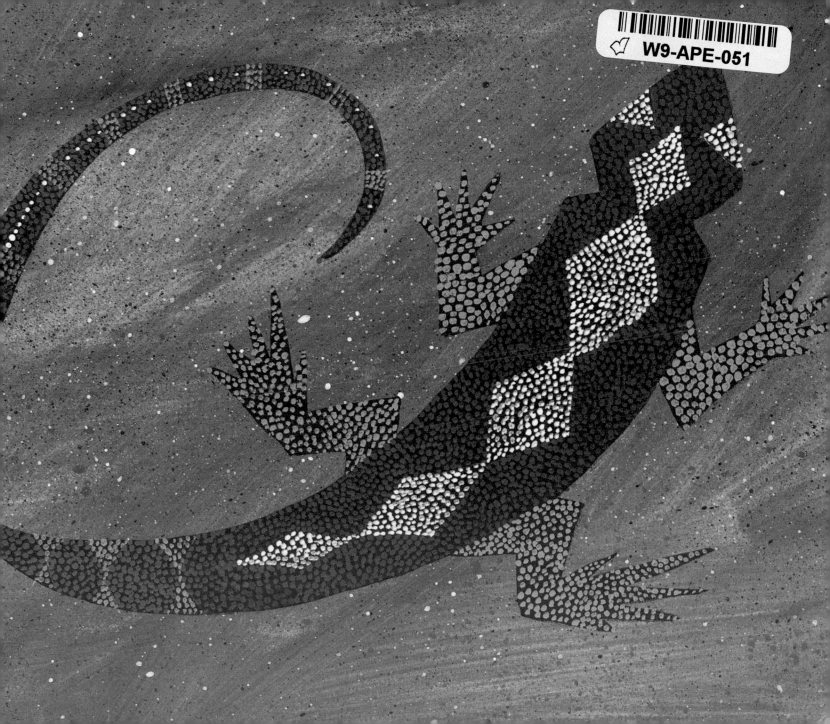

These pages and the next two show the actual size of a full-grown green iguana.

ALL ABOUT LIZARDS

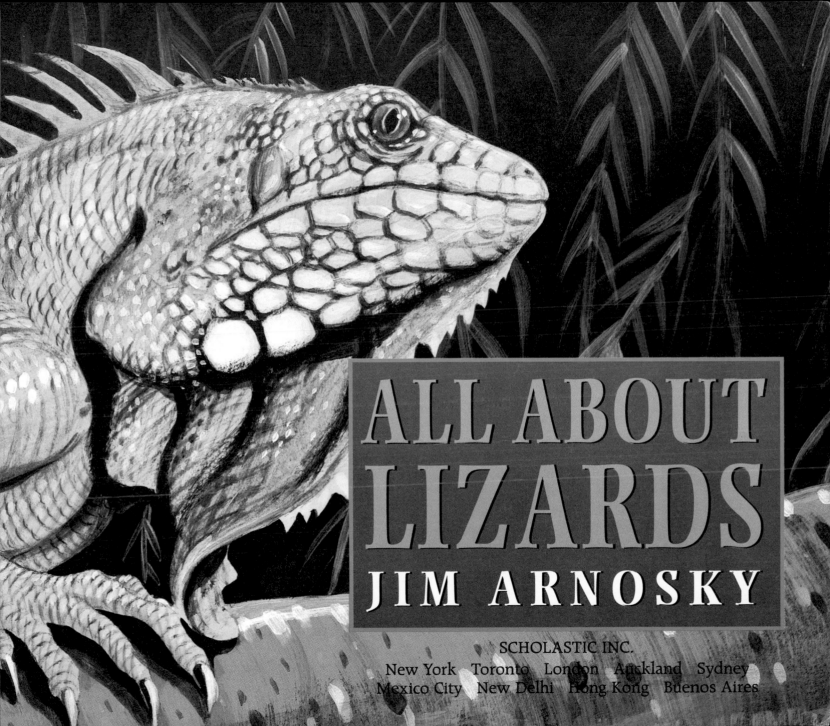

ALL ABOUT LIZARDS

JIM ARNOSKY

SCHOLASTIC INC.

New York   Toronto   London   Auckland   Sydney
Mexico City   New Delhi   Hong Kong   Buenos Aires

ISBN 0-590-48146-0

12 11 10 9 8 7 6   7 8 9/0

Printed in the U.S.A.
First printing, June 2004

The text type was set in Raleigh.
Jim Arnosky made these paintings
using acrylic paint on acid-free watercolor paper.

For
Darren
and Rex

◄ Chuckwalla

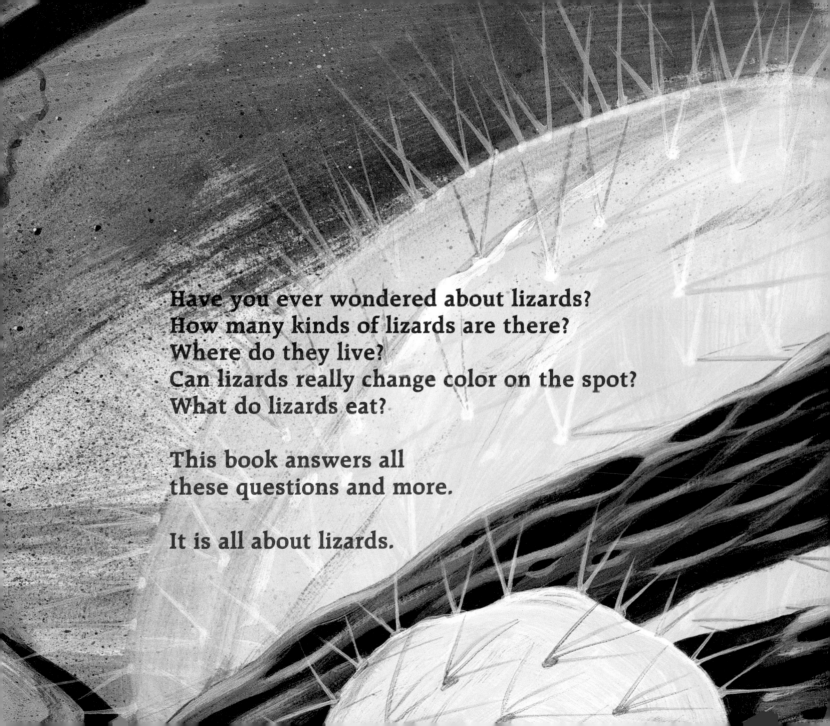

Have you ever wondered about lizards?
How many kinds of lizards are there?
Where do they live?
Can lizards really change color on the spot?
What do lizards eat?

This book answers all
these questions and more.

It is all about lizards.

◄ Marbled salamander

Snakes, turtles, alligators, crocodiles, and lizards are reptiles. Like all reptiles, lizards cannot regulate their body temperatures from within. To warm itself, a lizard moves to a warm place. To cool off, it finds shade. Most lizards live in warm climates. Those that live in colder climates hibernate during the coldest part of the year.

Of all reptiles, lizards are the most tolerant of extreme heat. On the hottest days, you will often find lizards out and about when other reptiles are lying low.

Salamanders resemble lizards but they are amphibians, not reptiles.

Green iguana ➤

American alligator ▼

So far, more than 3,000 species of lizards have been discovered in the world. The species vary in size, habits, and habitats. The lizards on this page are those most commonly seen in the United States.

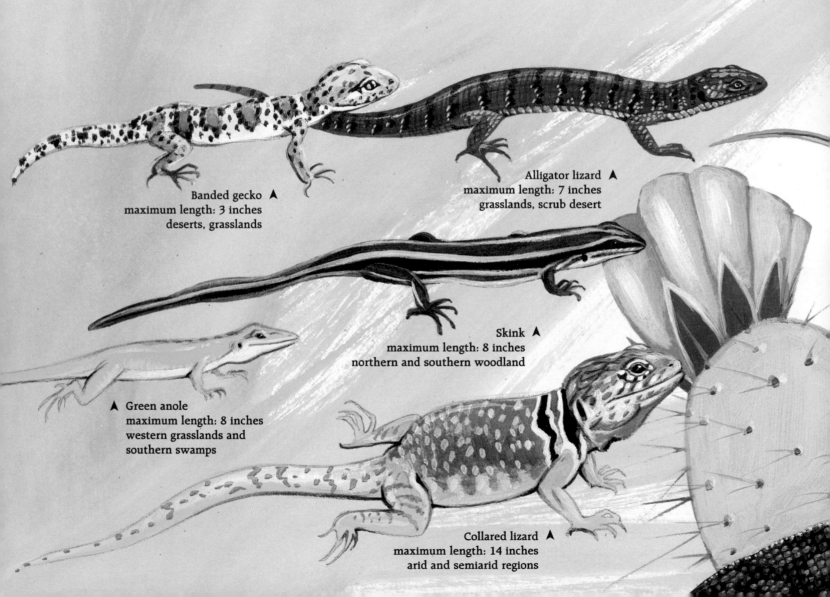

Banded gecko ⋀
maximum length: 3 inches
deserts, grasslands

Alligator lizard ⋀
maximum length: 7 inches
grasslands, scrub desert

Skink ⋀
maximum length: 8 inches
northern and southern woodland

⋀ Green anole
maximum length: 8 inches
western grasslands and
southern swamps

Collared lizard ⋀
maximum length: 14 inches
arid and semiarid regions

Side-blotched lizard
maximum length: 4 inches
arid and semiarid regions

Spiny lizard (fence lizard)
maximum length: 7 inches
fences and old buildings
in semiarid regions

Earless lizard
maximum length: 7 inches
semiarid regions

Six-lined racerunner (whiptail lizard)
maximum length: 10 inches
arid regions, grasslands, wetlands

Horned lizard
maximum length: 4 inches
arid and semiarid regions

Chuckwalla
maximum length: 15 inches
arid regions, especially rocky areas

Gila monster
maximum length: 15 inches
arid regions, especially grassy areas

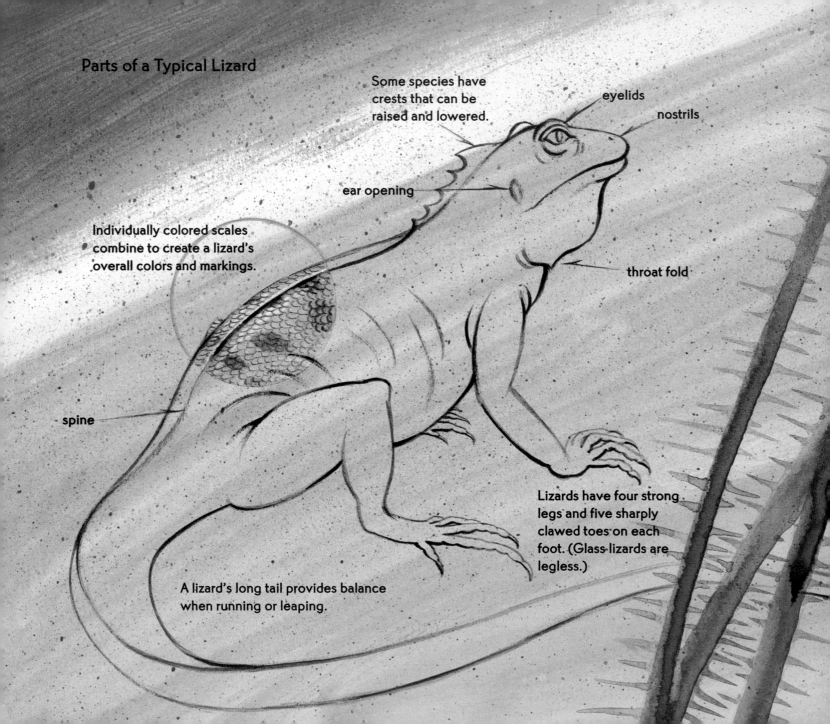

Parts of a Typical Lizard

Some species have crests that can be raised and lowered.

eyelids

nostrils

ear opening

Individually colored scales combine to create a lizard's overall colors and markings.

throat fold

spine

Lizards have four strong legs and five sharply clawed toes on each foot. (Glass lizards are legless.)

A lizard's long tail provides balance when running or leaping.

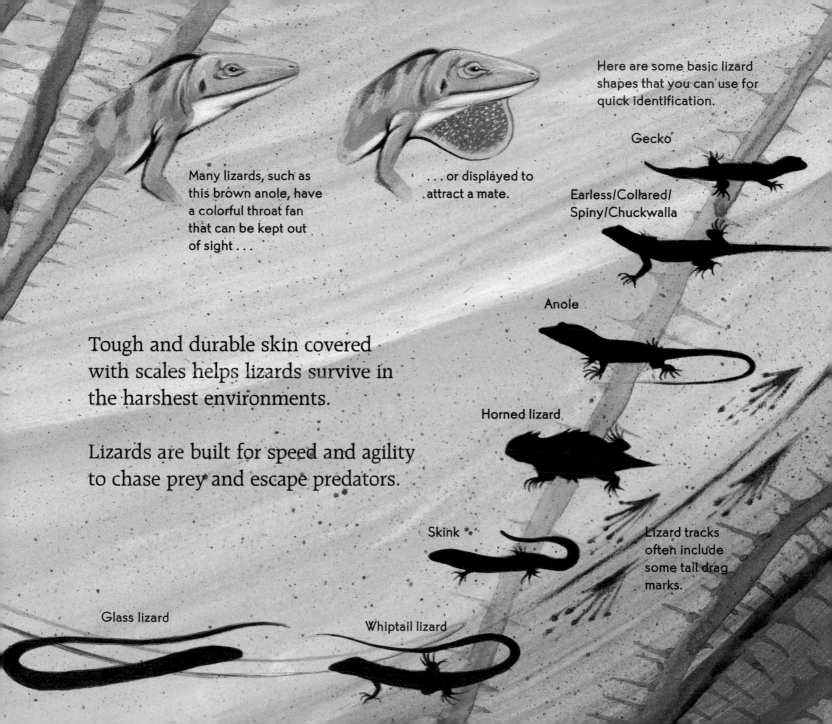

Many lizards, such as this brown anole, have a colorful throat fan that can be kept out of sight . . .

. . . or displayed to attract a mate.

Here are some basic lizard shapes that you can use for quick identification.

Gecko

Earless/Collared/Spiny/Chuckwalla

Anole

Tough and durable skin covered with scales helps lizards survive in the harshest environments.

Lizards are built for speed and agility to chase prey and escape predators.

Horned lizard

Skink

Lizard tracks often include some tail drag marks.

Glass lizard

Whiptail lizard

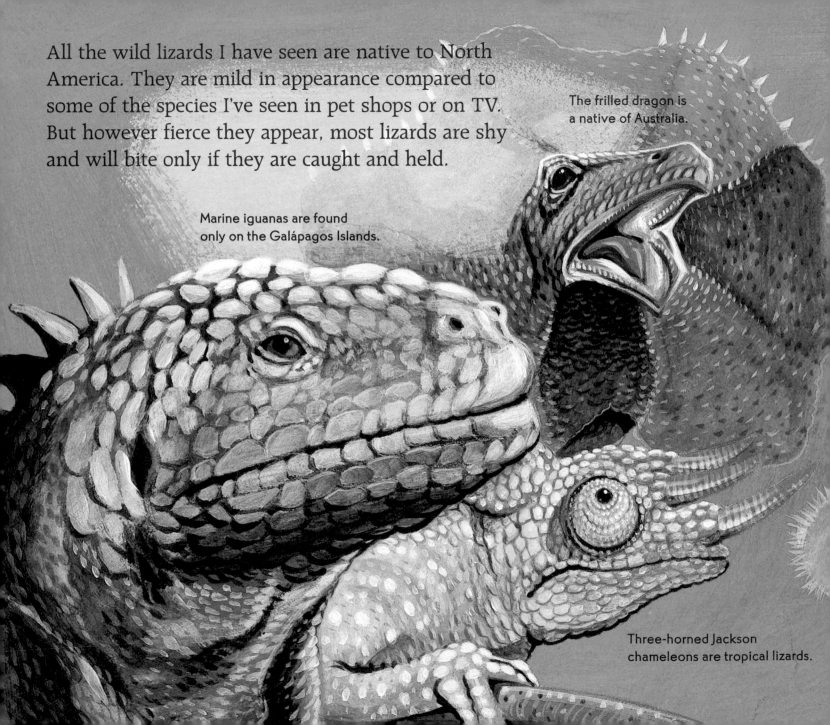

All the wild lizards I have seen are native to North America. They are mild in appearance compared to some of the species I've seen in pet shops or on TV. But however fierce they appear, most lizards are shy and will bite only if they are caught and held.

The frilled dragon is a native of Australia.

Marine iguanas are found only on the Galápagos Islands.

Three-horned Jackson chameleons are tropical lizards.

The only venomous lizards in the world are the Gila monsters of the Southwestern United States and their close relatives, the Mexican beaded lizards. The venom is primarily used to paralyze mice, birds, smaller lizards, and other prey. Though rarely fatal to humans, a bite from either of these lizards is extremely painful.

Gila monster ➤

The Gila monster and the Mexican beaded lizard are also the only lizards covered with shiny beadlike scales.

The largest living lizard, growing to a gigantic
12 feet in length, is the Komodo dragon. They are
found only on the island of Komodo, in Indonesia.
Komodo dragons are in the monitor lizard family.
All monitor lizards are carnivores. They eat fish,
water birds, and rodents. Komodo dragons even
prey on cattle, inflicting a bacteria-laden bite
that eventually weakens the animal for the kill.

This picture shows the actual size of the head of a Komodo dragon. It was painted from a life-size statue of a Komodo dragon.

Some scientists think that birds, not lizards, are the true descendants of the dinosaurs. I don't know. What do you think?

This collared lizard will search high and low for a suitable rock crevice in which to lay her 4 to 24 eggs.

For most species of lizards, life begins in an egg. Egg-bearing females deposit their eggs in hidden places. Shallow holes dug in sand, rock crevices, under rotting logs, and beneath leaf litter are all places where lizards may lay their eggs.

Lizard eggs are flexible, so they can stretch as the embryos inside develop and grow.

▼ Green iguana egg

Banded gecko egg ▲

The size of lizard eggs varies according to species.

The number of eggs a lizard lays depends on the species and size of the individual producing the eggs. Some lizards may only produce one egg. Some lay 31 eggs. All lizards abandon their eggs, leaving the hatchlings to fend for themselves.

When the baby lizard is fully formed, it chews its way out of the leathery egg.

Then, after shedding its tender newborn skin, the baby lizard instinctively begins to search for its very first meal, most likely some small insects.

shed skin

Throughout its life, each time a lizard experiences new growth, it will shed a skin.

Some large iguanas are strictly vegetarians. Others, such as the Gila monster and other powerful predatory lizards are primarily meat eaters. But most lizards eat a wide variety of foods, including:

spiders

worms

insects

other small lizards

snails

When lizards are eating, they remain quite still and it is not easy to find them. I look for small but obvious lumps on top of boulders.

This lump turned out to be a small lizard gobbling down a spider.

The quick dash is a lizard specialty.

The combination of sudden bursts of speed and camouflage coloring makes it possible for lizards to ambush and catch their food and to escape becoming food for larger predators.

Large, heavily scaled lizards such as this Australian blue-tongued skink have dark stripes and blotches that blend with grasses, stems, or pebbly ground. They rely solely on their markings for camouflage.

Anoles do not have bold markings to camouflage them. They simply change color to match their surroundings. A green anole can leap from a green leaf to a brown stem and change its color to brown in seconds.

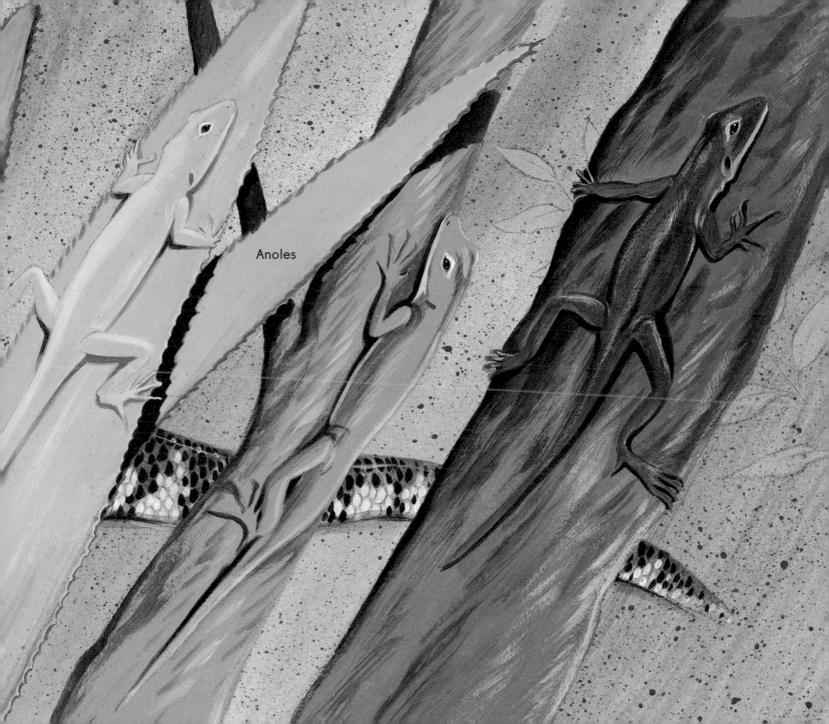

Anoles

Great egret with a skink

No matter how fast they can run or how well they can hide, lots of lizards still get caught. Lizards are an important source of food for many animals, such as snakes and birds. In the face of so many enemies, a lizard has one last means of escape. If it gets caught by the tail, a lizard can quickly break away and leave its tail behind.

A new, somewhat misshapen tail will grow as the lizard lives on.

Here is where the break occurs. Losing its tail to a predator makes a lizard less agile.

I have found lizards on stone walls, on
fence rails, in swamps, by the sea, on
tropical islands, at the edges of canyon
cliffs, and on the rocky desert floor. And
every lizard I have seen has
seen me first.

Many lizards live among us. They scoot across our footpaths and driveways. Lively and fun to watch, lizards make good neighbors.

Chuckwallas at dusk

MEET JIM ARNOSKY

JIM ARNOSKY is the author and illustrator of more than 70 books for children. Jim visited many parts of the United States looking for lizards. He made sketches in his notebook and took photographs and shot video. As Jim says in this book, he never once saw a lizard that didn't see him first!

When he is not traveling to visit schools and explore nature, Jim Arnosky lives in Vermont, with his wife, Deanna. There he fishes, hikes, writes, and paints. He also plays guitar and conga drum!

All About Lizards is the last book in the All About . . . series. The other titles are *All About Frogs*, *All About Owls*, *All About Turkeys*, *All About Alligators*, *All About Deer*, *All About Turtles*, *All About Rattlesnakes*, and *All About Sharks*.